GET SERIOUS: New & Selected Poems

previous Chax Press books by Jefferson Carter:

Sentimental Blue
My Kind of Animal

*Bonnie,
thanks for being
such a good pen pal!*

GET SERIOUS

NEW & SELECTED POEMS

Jefferson Carter

chax press 2013

Copyright © 2013 Jefferson Carter. All rights reserved.
ISBN 0 925904 20 1

Acknowledgments

Grateful acknowledgment is made to the following publications in which some of these poems first appeared, often in slightly different versions: *Barrow Street, Cream City Review, Cutthroat, Merge, New Poets of the American West, Sandscript, Sonora Review, Spork, 10X3 Plus, The Missing Fez, The Tucson Poet, Tucson Weekly, 2River View,* and *Whetstone.*

Thanks to my friends on The Boathouse,

*to my poetry-pals Michael Gessner, Steven Salmoni,
and Tim Schaffner,*

and dedicated, as always, to Connie and to Evan.

NEW POEMS

Stone Loop	11
Grindstone	12
Study of Three Pears	13
Mockingbird	14
American Ingenuity	15
Fried Green Beans	16
An Apology for Wannabes	17
"Marley"	19
Freeze	20
Taming Texas	21
Bilagaana Dream	22
Puma	23
Nature was My Church	24
Kill Data	25
Victim Poetry	26
Classism	27
Letter to a Young Poet	28
Cool	29
Hard-wired	30
Blame Sutra	31
Pasture	32
Sunlight	33
King Onela's Dog	34
Lapland	35
Mall	36
Dirty Old Men	37
Arbitrary	38
Mormon Houses	39
Memento Mori	40
Whereabouts	41
Amulet	42
There's No Such Thing as a Stupid Question	43
Cat Pose	44

SELECTED POEMS

A Centaur	47
Johnny-Jump-Up	48
Strep Throat	49
Puerto Peñasco	50
Maria's Paragraph	51
My First Love	52
Finally, a Love Poem for My Wife	53
Vest	54
Litter Box	55
Thunder	57
Otis	58
Please	59
Exemplar	60
How to Live with Teens	61
Writing in the Shower	62
Vanity Western	63
A Reading	65
Land of the Pharaohs	66
Reception	67
Starry Night	68
Elavil	69
Like	70
Trail Ride	71
The Sanctificationist of Ajo	72
The Oral Tradition	73
Abu Ghraib (A True Story)	74
Don't Get Me Started	75
China Exhibit	77
Steam	78
The Mummy	79
The First Saltist Church of Tariq Our Lord	80
My Prayer	81
Washing Machine	82
What I Did in Heaven	83
Helen	84

NEW POEMS

STONE LOOP

That trite motif
of class conflict, a job
at the dollar store, no more
whimsey, just the modest truth
of a found phrase, "Roller
Coaster Road" or "Stone Loop."
Where was I? Not
in the middle of my life,
not like Dante entering
the profound wood. More like
a sit-down comedian, a communist
allergic to theory, a retired
bobsledder playing
ping-pong with his wife.

GRINDSTONE

Oh, buffcollared nightjar,
little nipple cactus, oh,
superb beardtongue,

forgive my periods
of intense folding
& faulting. I peel

the organic label
off the apple & stick it
on the cat's head.

He squints at me,
buzzing & chirping like
a broken Geiger counter.

At the end of "America,"
Ginsberg vows to put
his queer shoulder

to the wheel. Online,
an old photo, a joke,
someone in a wool suit

pressing his face
to the grindstone
he pretends to turn.

STUDY OF THREE PEARS

I grip the stem of the pear
between my teeth & pull it out
like the pin of a grenade.
What a fucked-up decade!
Last century, during peacetime,
Stevens described two pears,
immortalizing citron. He swore
the pears resembled nothing else.
What a difference 26,280 days make,
15,137,280 little hours! I slice
the pear in half, spoon out the seeds
& walk onto the porch, eating,
a bonfire on every lawn & down
the road, the body of a dog hanging
head-down from the power lines.

MOCKINGBIRD

Our third president owned
a pet mockingbird named Dick.
Let's not mention what else
he owned. Dick dug Monticello,
that big white layer cake.
He'd click & chatter. He'd mimic
the field slaves' hosannahs
until he'd almost faint, wobbling
on his perch like a double
handful of dirty cotton.

AMERICAN INGENUITY

After a buffalo burger
& some butter lettuce,
triple-washed, I'm ready
to refinance the house.
I can't sleep nights,
coveting the sudden wealth
of someone like Ragged Dick
the bootblack, a fictional
character, but still. . . .

I'd vote Socialist. I can't sleep,
concocting get-rich-quick schemes:
a great-tasting colonoscopy prep.
Or *Hasta* Yoga, copywriting,
like Mr. Bikram, ancient *asanas*,
the ones that stretch wrist & fingers,
yoga for signatories. I'd vote
Socialist. My best idea yet,
lavender-scented formaldehyde.

FRIED GREEN BEANS

The perfect protein, deep-fried green beans
at our favorite restaurant. I ate them
all, my wife still mad at bedtime
because I didn't play the scene from
"Lady & the Tramp," nudging some beans
with my nose in her direction. Breaking
our promise never to go to bed angry,
she smokes on the porch & I fall asleep.

I'm wearing a canvas duster, a cast iron
replica of a Colt .45 like an anchor in my pocket.
Three Yaqui kids, wearing red headbands
and black Metallica t-shirts, chainsaw past
on rusty ATVs. The last boy turns
& before I can wave goodbye, shoots me
in the stomach. The horizon a line of fire,
I wake up, my wife asking me what's wrong?

AN APOLOGY FOR WANNABES

Not one Apache
in this audience
listening to the
bearded white man
tell stories
about Cochise.
Easy irony? I know,
& some of us are
wearing Geronimo
Homeland Security t-shirts
& yes, all of us
are sweating
like converts trying
to imagine
that shining camp
upon the hill
or a raiding party
trotting down Wall Street.

In this Age
of Irony, let me,
as one of our
political sock puppets
used to say, let me
say this about that—
without us,
the lessons you

learn from history
would be noisy
as a marching band
& empty as a Kleenex box
on the table
outside some senator's
office door.

"MARLEY"

It's not just the ganja
talking, the subtitles suggest
an urgent communication
from outer space, a message
for our own good. When asked
about his many children
& his seven other women,
he half-sings "I obey Jah's laws."
Cool. Whatever. I know
I can't cram any more
into the long-term storage unit
I call my brain, no room
for the crate of bobble hats
& spliffs, for the granite Lion
of Judah, the needlepoint
portrait of Halie Salassie,
the easy chairs and ratty sofas
of faith, but I can see him,
transfigured, damp & glowing,
raising over his backlit dreads
the dry clasped hands
of the two white politicians,
singing his message,
"One Love" or whatever
it is, without subtitles.

FREEZE

The owners of the B & B across
the street have draped old bedsheets
over their roses. Each bush huddles
beneath its threadbare cloak, one
pastel blue, one pink, one green
& one pale yellow, like squaws
in a bad southwestern painting
titled *Little Powwow*, titled
Maidens in the Snow, four figures
beside the path to the nervous fort.

TAMING TEXAS

Jingling their spurs,
cocking their rifles,
the *Diablos Tejanos*
evolved into politicians
& golfers who'd steal two
horse-buckets of whiskey
before you could say
remember those stout,
red-necked women
the Comanche bands raped
& dragged through forests
of prickly-pear, torn
beyond recognition?
Look at those weed-infested
parade grounds & tell me
men enjoy discipline more
than vengeance, our
moving spirit. At least,
we got elbow room.
Little tourist infrastructure,
I salute you as you expand
in the presence
of god's sunshine & his
absolute bliss. *Pendejo!*

BILAGAANA DREAM
for Sherwin Bitsui

In my dream last night,
you loaned me your old pickup
& sat beside me, speaking only
when spoken to, your aura,
if I believed in auras, a steady
diamond light. I talked & talked
& talked like a *bilagaana* sitcom,
recalling how my father restored
antique electric chairs, oiling the straps
& polishing the helmets while I poured
vodka into the hummingbird feeders
so they wouldn't freeze. My introduction
to Mother Earth. Someday, tell me
about yours. I woke up, four pink
dust devils in the corner of my eye.

PUMA

The cat purrs
in the crook of my arm,
his gray face silver-edged
against the gray fleece
of my pajama sleeve.
I wonder what he sees,
his yellow eyes blinking
slowly. Today at work,
remote camera 5 recorded
a sequence of images,
a female puma, staring
at the flash, then flirting
with it, lying down & rolling
over, waving paws like
oven mitts, 120-pound
house cat, the same
merciless, yellow eyes.

NATURE WAS MY CHURCH

Just when you thought it was safe
to idealize again, to abandon yourself
to something pure & unequivocal,
you learned more from the African Lion
Rescue Project. You learned
how the new king hunts down all
the old king's cubs & severs their spines.

Animal, vegetable or mineral? This time
you choose mineral, dumb & deaf
as the Whatever Stone, that souvenir
from Africa your friends' dinner guests
absently finger as they discuss the future
of NPR or the possible correlations
between table talk & ethnic cleansing.

KILL DATA

My soap, cruelty-free,
hand-crafted, contains
olive oil. I smell

like a salad. Do Muslim
men do household chores?
I consider converting.

Did their ancestors, like
ours, keep kill data?

"After mass, December 23,
1940, Santa Cruz River,
a jaguar, male, roped,
killed with rocks, 138 lbs,
tail 72 inches, stomach
full of frogs." Can you
even say this in Arabic?

VICTIM POETRY

Cliterature just rejected
my latest poems.
It's three P.M.
& I go back to bed.
I wake to the sound
of gospel-sized hail.
I go back to sleep,
my new Posturepedic
mattress, custom-made
for a bad back & thin skin,
so comfy you'll never
get up again.

CLASSISM
      for Linh Dinh

Yes, maybe they are
"cadavers," your word
after seven beers
when you'd glimpsed
your audience. Yes,
they're wearing silk ties
& tasselled loafers.
Would bib overalls
be better? Or dirty
fingernails? Just be your
sunny, foul-mouthed self.
Here's your chance,
yes, here's your chance
to knock the dead dead.

LETTER TO A YOUNG POET

"She got brown sugar
all over her booger wooger."

I can't believe Bob Marley wrote that
either. I'm a mimic & can feel

myself itching. What else rhymes
with sugar? Not much.

The lyricists know songs
please easier than poetry.

Your new poem, the one
that begins "All you self-righteous

foot-fetishists"? Set to music,
you could get away with it.

My advice? Stay playful,
even childish. Try not to yearn

so much for steel drums, a funky
bass & his master's voice.

COOL

Nobody says "Go, cat, go"
anymore. I miss that.
You're lucky to hear,
during those outbursts,
those passionate solos,
a laid-back "cool," pronounced
"kuel" by someone majoring in
international pharmacology
or art as the history
of decoration. Look!
Ornamental ironwork
on a screen door, what very
well could be an anteater
barking at the moon.

HARD-WIRED

I heard Mick Jagger's got
a small penis. I heard Anne Waldman
recite her 900-page feminist epic,
The Iovis Trilogy. A friend suggested
a lapel pin, a crown of thorns, for anyone
who finishes it. I bought a copy,
glued the middle pages, then cut out
a hiding place for my new 9 mm.
Don't tell. I'm off to the moisture farm.
I registered for a workshop
titled "Shuffling Off This Moral Coil,"
where I'll confess to thoughts like
"You be the dancer, I'll be the pole."

BLAME SUTRA

I blame yoga, no, not yoga, I blame
Buddhism. In Sanskrit, "modesty"
means not calling attention to yourself.
In American, "poetry" means calling
attention to yourself. When I perform
(or "preform," as the racing program
misspells it, "see the Budweiser Clydesdales
preform"), when I perform my poems,
I want to clap a hand over my mouth.
Shut the fuck up & let someone else talk!
Those ghosts & mannequins around you,
they all have a tale to tell. If you listen,
you'll hear the breath that breathes us all.
Don't & you'll make jokes like this: in Texas,
foreplay means asking, "you awake?"

PASTURE

To a narcissist, all
the world's a mirror.
The day I misread
the no trespassing sign
in the laundromat window
as no trepanning, I retired
from narcissism. I stopped
worrying about my headaches.
I'm not so lonely now
& even a goat isn't just
a goat. I told my neighbor
my lawn's a pasture & today
I saw a herd, fainting goats
he calls them, grazing there.

SUNLIGHT

I remember lying
on Nancy's bed,
Nancy on one side,
her older sister
on the other, sunlight
warming our bare legs
as I recited my new poem.
I remember thinking
I love women, the way
they smell, how they look
& feel, the nightclub
of my mind quiet for once,
the poem describing
a sentient rock, a hermit
who sealed up the entrance
to his cave, leaving a slit
through which the villagers
pushed his food.

KING ONELA'S DOG

The Beowulf poet sang
about "A balm in bed
to the battle-scarred Swede."
Some scholar translated
"balm in bed" as "sleeping
companion," identifying
this companion as King Onela's
favorite dog, not his queen,
but you know scholars, anything
to get published. A dog's nose
is 100 times more sensitive
than a man's. The Great Hall,
unwashed bodies, animal skins,
chamber pots under the table,
guests, gorged, vomiting
onto the floor, ready for the
next course. To be a dog then
must have been very heaven!
Around 400 A.D. these dogs
got together & swore fealty to man,
to be his disco ball & best friend
forever. What did the dogs
get in return? All you can
eat, some glorious stinks & best
of all, the infinite loneliness
of the two-legged tribes.

LAPLAND

A wooden dog with real eyes
snuffled across the floor
of the lodge, wriggling his segments.

I ate raw horsemeat from a bowl.
Like a tourist, I saw some ceremonies,
watching from a hill young men leg-wrestling
in reindeer sweaters & leather aprons.

What I remember most
is the damp cedar
of the interiors & literally
sleeping with a flexible larva wearing
three pairs of red platform heels.

MALL

All those air-brushed models,
12-feet-tall, pouting & whispering,
"I'm beautiful. You're not."
I forgive my internal (I wanted
to say eternal) erection. We're
hard-wired to respond to beauty.
I don't forgive Victoria's Secret,
those poor teenage girls flip, flip,
flipping their straightened hair
or plucking at their skinny jeans,
plumbers' cracks & camel toes,
or giving this old man dirty looks
as if there's a thought balloon
over my head. I'm not being
flippant. What if love means never
having to say you're beautiful?

DIRTY OLD MEN

A good day.
A study involving
freezer bags, armpits,
nursing pads & jars,
a subject-driven day:

"Old men don't smell bad."

"Old men smell better
than their adult sons."

Befriend your breath.
Applaud today's guest ethicist.
Me? I'll sanctify the names
of those neuropsychologists
who today announced,

"The older a man gets,
the more he smells
like a rich woman."

ARBITRARY

I'm biking across campus,
wondering why two breasts?
Why not one like a whale
or eight like a dog? Why
two legs, walking upright?
Wouldn't we be happier
on all fours? No more
middle-aged back troubles
& we'd move at that slower pace
the gurus recommend.
We'd be kinder, balancing
on two knees and one hand
at an intersection, gesturing
to our fellow quadrupeds, "no,
please, you go first." It could
happen. Or I could say
to the coed jogging
in the bike lane, "Don't give me
the stink eye!" Everything's
so arbitrary. I could even tell her
someday she'll feel like me,
like a barely legal alien
on a stolen unicycle. Or not.

MORMON HOUSES

The penalty for bigamy is
two wives. Those old houses
on Speedway, slated for demolition,
they're not duplexes but "Mormon"
houses, a separate front door
for the other wife. A penalty?
Think of the permutations!
You go next door & discover
your two wives enjoying oral sex
on the second-best rug or, worse,
sitting at the kitchen table,
their garments damp, sharing
a bottle of coke. What do you
do now? The penalty is free will.
I admit Joseph Smith's seer stones
& the Angel Moroni are a bit much,
but all roads lead to Damascus,
I've been told. So how about a little
respect? What would I do? I hope
I'd say "You gals mind if I join you?"
as I smiled, opening my arms wide
like the Christ of Rio de Janeiro.

MEMENTO MORI

My wife's the best-looking person
at this party. I'm second-best.
Someone's bald mother slumps
in her wheelchair, surprised to be
a memento mori. Their arthritic feet
like satyrs' hooves, others keep
losing their flip-flops as they do
the mash-potato & sing "Do
You Love Me?" We don't need no
stinking paranormal urban fantasies,
but doesn't anyone want to leave
a good-looking corpse anymore?

All the poets my age are now
writing about death. No more
heavy-breathing, no more sexual healing
or swooning at life's infinite possibilities.
"Death," wrote the poet, "be not proud."
I'd like to add, "At least be stylish
or try to smell nice." Don't feel bad.
It's not you. It's the formaldehyde.

WHEREABOUTS

My friend, who dabbles
in anthropology, tells me
once women stood upright,
breasts evolved, resembling
buttocks to remind men
of the vagina's whereabouts.
I like these science-based stories
our politicians call fairy tales.
They believe God created Adam
in His image. Adam, in Hebrew,
means red dirt. I imagine Cain
looking up at that Scowl in the Sky
& turning on the radio. Tomorrow's
forecast: 10 % chance of grain.

AMULET

The vet calls it "extrusion" & prescribes
an antibiotic, room-temperature, as if the cat
cares. He'll lose that fang in a few weeks.
I ask the vet if she knows some place
that could gold-plate the tooth & hang it
on a silver chain, an amulet against
this evil century. She shrugs & glances
away as if I'm a Scientologist or mentally ill.
O, ye of little faith! The Mai Mai rebels
believed holy water changed the bullets
of the government troops into rain.
They brandished spears, wearing nothing
but shower caps on their heads & around
their necks, bath plugs for amulets.
Easy pose not easy no more. Nothing not
easy no more. But come, hang this cat's tooth
around your neck & see how much it helps.
The Mai Mai rebels? 20% almost survived.

THERE'S NO SUCH THING AS A STUPID
QUESTION

All the good questions have been asked.
Am I my brother's keeper?
Are you my pork chop?
What's a guy gotta do to get a drink around here?

I've been dreaming about my brother,
who lived on Crete. I dragged him out of the surf,
dead drunk, 150-pound carp, but hairier
& muttering every pariah's secret,
"I'm a creep. I'm a creep."

Do dreams begin responsibilities?
Can you sing *"Frère Jacques,*
Frère Jacques, dormez vous?"
A squalid rented room,
the furniture shrouded in wax paper.
Who's to blame? A stupid question.
Brother Jon, Jon, my brother, are you sleeping?

CAT POSE

My mat smells
like cat chow.

As that old song
"Somebody's Watching You"

doesn't say, nobody's
watching you.

Nobody's watching me
except both cats

napping on their chair
as I return to my breath,

preparing for corpse pose.
My teacher likes

"hospice" as a metaphor
for life. Why maim

each other? We're all
patients here.

SELECTED POEMS

From *None of This Will Kill Me* (Tucson: Moon Pony Press, 1987), *Tough Love* (West Chester, PA: Riverstone Poetry Press, 1993), *Homemade Arrows* (Tucson: Red Felt Publishing, 2000), *Litter Box* (Tucson: Spork Press, 2004), *Sentimental Blue* (Tucson: Chax Press, 2007), and *My Kind of Animal* (Tucson: Chax Press, 2010).

A CENTAUR

For laughs,
I imitate a horse,
lowering my bare shoulder
into the sand
of the arroyo, my wife
watching from above
& our son inside the blue backpack
watching while I roll, kicking
my hooves & neighing, husband
turned centaur, father
as some big animal.
The boy laughs
because his mother's laughing
& I lurch to my feet, shaking,
blowing through my nostrils,
feeling foolish,
but what's a family for?
Climbing back up,
I smell creosote & sage
& I understand the Greeks
who carried in their armor
a bag of spices
that smelled like home.

(1987)

JOHNNY-JUMP-UP

Leaping inside the Johnny-Jump-Up,
a twisting bag of houndstooth check
like the pants of a winter visitor,
my son giggles as I bend my body
into position three of *Surya
Namaskara*, the salutation
to the sun. I breathe as if I believe
yoga will make me young, a faith like
letters to the editor or small checks
mailed to an honest politician. Too
skeptical to chant *Om shanti shanti*,
I stop & kiss my laughing son, breathing
his odor, a sweetness the world once had.

(1987)

STREP THROAT

I sleep in my son's bed,
his comforter billowing
over me like meringue,
the poems of Che Guevara
under my pillow.
When my wife comes home,
she lets the dog in,
the dog who loves me
unconditionally. What did
Che call his apolitical friends?
Drunks, singing, their throats
about to be cut. The dog
loves me for myself, morose,
apolitical, the tang of penicillin
on my skin & he scuttles
down the hall, wondering
where I am, finally
wriggling the comforter
aside & draping himself
over my head like
someone's flung beret.

(2000)

PUERTO PEÑASCO

The screen window
is a grid across the stars.
Two strands of steel
quarter Venus. Her
counterpart, smoking Delicados
in the old hotel down the beach,
taps a key against her glass.
By the time light
from that planet reaches her,
she'll be gone
& the fishing boats
will be pulling the burning
chandeliers out to sea.

(1993)

MARIA'S PARAGRAPH

I had a
real nice person
but in this moment
is not here.
I will like him
to come back
but most want
that can't have.
Most want
but I can't
have it with me
no more. Someday
this strange thing
happened to me
that I thought that
I was in love
with this person
but then I can't talk
to this person see
at his eyes. So days
pass but right away
I say no at him. So
two weeks pass, yes
I wanted. So
two years pass
& most want, most
want that can't have.
(1993)

MY FIRST LOVE

You bitched about my kisses,
too tentative, like one
of those toy birds dipping
its beak into a glass of water.
You're coming to visit me
& my wife. Who wants to hear
Etta sing "The Jealous Kind"?
I used sex to stay on top.
Once I compared
an old lover's nipples
to tiny sombreros & you
looked at me with such pity
I felt myself disappear.

(2007)

FINALLY, A LOVE POEM FOR MY WIFE

You're my sticky mat, my
power anthem, my vertebrae
like pearls on a string,
one at a time. You read me
letters to the editor, news
from the parallel universe:
"Simply look at the man
who is our president, see
a good man, with a good heart."
You tell me funny stories,
someone's son explaining he
can't watch gratuitous violence
but he can watch historical
violence. Or some kid defining
the parts of speech: Lungs. Air.
You're my lungs, my air.

(2007)

VEST

A pocket wobbles down the street.
Someone picks it up & takes it home.
What's more hopeful than a pocket
without a coat? I bragged I could
move in an hour, two cardboard boxes
& all my earthly goods But you get
married, have a kid or two, pretty soon
stuff owns you as the dead comedian said.
Today I walked in on my wife, naked
in the bathroom, me, not the wife, wearing
nothing but my down vest. I felt sexy,
the pillowy gray nylon hiding my bad parts.
I flexed the good parts, my guns. What's
sexier than bare arms & a sleeveless vest?
My wife laughed & said I looked gay.
That's ok. I never thought I'd be sleeping with a
60-year-old woman either. An old Dean
of Students once told us freshmen, I can
turn my wife into a quivering blob of protoplasm
in ten seconds. I remember how we gagged.

(2010)

LITTER BOX

My wife asked me this morning
if I'd ever cheated on her.
My ex-wife called this afternoon
& asked me the same thing.
What's going on?
That new Italian movie
the art film crowd adores,
the characters hysterical, nearly
operatic, their marriages dead
or dying. I imagine all the couples
sipping cappuccinos after the movie,
nibbling biscotti, that close
to confessing their own infidelities.
I love my wife. I don't whine
about my latest chore, cleaning
the litter box four or five times
a day. I can imagine one
of those histrionic Italian husbands
fuming, yearning for his mistress
as he kneels by the reeking box,
scooping cat feces & urinous clots
of litter into a plastic bag.
The second I'm done, our old cat
comes running. Otherwise,
he limps from room to room, moaning
like the ghost of some animal

whose bladder burst.
I love that old cat. Most nights
he snuggles under the comforter,
buzzing between me & my wife like a
space heater I need to repair.

(2004)

THUNDER

Lightning, then, of course, thunder.
We can get used to anything.
The window, lit up, shakes
& we're comforted, pulling
the blankets to our chins. The dog,
half-blind, diabetic, fat as a woodchuck,
burrows between us, panting,
trembling like she's never heard
thunder before. Maybe she hasn't,
she lives so much in the moment.
Here's her day: I was in. Now I'm out.
I was out. Now I'm in. You going
to eat that? You going to eat that?
I'll eat that! Here's her night so far:
What's that? Thunder. What's that?
Thunder. What's that? Thunder.

(2007)

OTIS

The vet opens our dog's mouth
& shows us the gray mass on his palate,
the tumor that's grown so big
his breath whistles through one nostril.
Our options — $6000 for radiation
or do nothing. Goddamn anyone
who denies him a soul. My wife squats
beside him on the linoleum floor,
crooning as he whistles into her palm.

(2010)

PLEASE

I wake up,
eye-to-eye with the cat's anus.
He's purring on my chest.
Why me, oh, Lord?
Like face time
with a rusty washer.
I hear good things
about the ungulates,
their table manners, their
clean plates. My kind
of animal, sweet-smelling,
modest, not like cats
weaving between your legs,
scent glands under their tails,
rubbing until you smell
like them, safe enough
to love. Take my species,
for example. I'm a person,
p-e-r-s-o-n. Before
the plague of white-eyes,
each nation called itself
"the people." Take
my species. Please.

(2010)

EXEMPLAR

I can't believe I'm telling my son
about the good old days, my travels
& sexual conquests. He pretends
he's not listening, then says that's disgusting.
I agree. Staying with Cornelia in Augsburg,
visiting her family, her mother who didn't
understand why the Allies bombed Munich,
the horizon burning, her father, a one-legged
shadow who escaped through his study window
when company knocked. I wasn't company,
more like a plague visited upon them, eating
their food, speaking English, fucking their daughter
every night in her childhood bed, doggy-style,
staring at the mandala between my thumbs,
sometimes thinking take that & that & that
because it felt so good & because no one
ever mentioned Nazis or the Jews. Better
left unsaid, these stories, these examples
I set for my son, who keeps saying
that's disgusting, that's so disgusting.

(2000)

HOW TO LIVE WITH TEENS

James Wright, that famous poet
nobody reads anymore, wrote
"When I was a boy
I loved my country. . . .
Hell, I ain't got nothing.
Ah, you bastards,
How I hate you." He also said
"Mad means something."
Tell me about it!
Cowboy karaoke enrages my son.
Those punk rockers last night?
He says they're shit
musicians. I say they're not
like James Wright. They'd be pissed off
in Paradise. Parents, listen!
If we didn't talk about music,
we wouldn't talk at all.

(2004)

WRITING IN THE SHOWER

I wanted something
Eastern European, you know,
something portentous
in the best sense of the word,
But what I managed was
two lines of southwestern
animal husbandry, half
a simile comparing
something wet to a teaser
stallion on a stud farm
& I was too busy
to mention the sow bugs
in the shower stall,
which echoed like a school
for famous readers.

(2000)

VANITY WESTERN

How not to write
a sex scene: "Next
came her bloomers.
She stood before him, a
fully naked adult woman.
They both got into the bedroll
for a night of sexual
satisfaction to both parties."

Go ahead. Laugh.
Here's his disclaimer:
"The author intends no
harm or injury to anyone."

He wants me to edit
his next western. I just might.
I'd correct his punctuation
but edit all that inchoate
love? No way.

He sent me a photo
of the winner's circle,
his scruffy bay colt, his
daughters beaming & there,
behind the grandchildren,

someone he just met, me.
His wife on one side, him
on the other, their arms
around my waist.

(2007)

A READING
> "An eland. Look, an eland!" –Randall Jarrell

We're all sitting here, screwing
the caps off bottled tap water.
That's right, tap water, expressed
in plastic that leaches. Are we
stupid or what? The crème
de la crème, the postmodern,
the concerned, the anti-Amuricans.
We'd better wise up or we'll end up
writing sonnets, Italian sonnets
with only four different sounds,
pain, brain, you, few, scorch, gone.
We don't even know our even-toed
ungulates, that the common eland
& the giant eland are the same.

(2010)

LAND OF THE PHARAOHS

I like being called "brother"
by black men. I like walking past
Land of the Pharaohs
& being invited in by the brothers
to bless them with a poem.
"Brothers," I say, "brothers,
please, no keyboards, no congas,
let me lay something white & uptight
on you brothers." I recite my poem
about Martians & Geiger counters,
its conclusion an ironic invitation
to Jesus to drop by some morning
for coffee. They hate it.
The brothers hate it
but they're polite, not like Kerouac
at the Living Theater,
heckling Frank O'Hara
or the Academy Awards audience
mocking poor Sally Fields
when she said "You
like me! You really do
like me!" The brothers forgive me
as they'd forgive a flying nun
who alighted among them
& roosted, preening, while a brother
recited his hip-hop poem called
"Kill the White Muthafuckers."

(2004)

RECEPTION
for Jim Waid

I've been thinking about white cake
all day. Every woman I talk to
at the reception has bad breath.

You know, you try to be polite
but you just want to press a hand
over her mouth. My psychiatrist

says it's me, not them, a side effect
of the drug. What do I say
to the nice woman confiding in me,

her breath like rotting meat?
It's not you, it's me? If
wishes were horses, I'd buy

that big painting, a lustrous wall
titled "Haven," so big I'd have to
knock out my interior walls,

weight-bearing or not. Someone laughs
& says be careful what you wish for.
He'd starve if not for week-old bread

& art openings. He's here for the food.

(2010)

STARRY NIGHT

We went to Dee's for dinner
& I got into her medicine cabinet.
I floated through dessert
like a starry night. My internist,
a good guy, really, but he wears
these beads & tells stupid jokes.
I kept dropping hints—
I pee all night. I break things.
I forgot a jacket somewhere.
Would Valium help? Or
something stronger? He acts
like I'm Van Gogh waving
a butter knife. Remember
Joni Mitchell? How she
kidded around? Hey, man,
do "Starry Night" again, man.

(2000)

ELAVIL

Every family has that story
about grandpa getting blue
& going to bed for a month,
curtains drawn. When I get blue,
it's no joke. Ask a Mormon
missionary how he feels,
bugging housewives, wiping
spit off his shoes. Elavil
online, one-hundred dollars
for thirty caps. Possible side effects–
black tongue, breast development
in males, coma, hives,
strange taste, swollen testicles,
stroke, vomiting, red
or purple spots on skin.
How low can you go? How high
can you get? Me? When I'm happy,
I sign all my e-mails X0X0X0.

(2007)

LIKE

I like that expression
"the bruised earth" better
than that old chestnut
"the bruise-colored sky."
Words matter. What if
Winona's parents named her
"Barstow" or "Gallup"?
Would her ears still be famous?
Would they still dominate
the big screen like satellite dishes,
like incarnations of that song
"Little Wing"? Sometimes
I forget "pop" means "popular,"
not "short-lived" as in "poof,"
now you see it, now you don't.
Here's, like, a funny passage
from a popular novel: "I like
the clouds," somebody offers.
"They're, like, a metaphor."
"They are a metaphor," I point out.
"If they were like a metaphor,
they'd be, like, a simile." O.K.
Let's get serious now. Let's,
like, return to the bruised earth.

(2010)

TRAIL RIDE

Between mesquite & the scraped dirt
of the building sites, our horses plod,
nose to tail. My wife's on Cimarron,
I'm on Dakota, their stable names probably
"horse" or "move over." What a life.
Dakota's so wide, my thighs ache.
The wrangler keeps looking back,
making sure we're o.k. My wife's o.k.
She loves that slowpoke Cimarron,
she loves the ravens overhead, the doves
calling from the desert broom.

What do I love? I used to tell my son
how I'd ride bareback, snapping
my homemade arrows at jackrabbits.
I hope I love something more than comfort.
I hook one sore leg over the saddle horn.
The wrangler looks back & gapes. My wife
tells me later I looked like a crazy old
woman, riding sidesaddle, wearing
worn red boots, some old lady, comfortable
nowhere, slapping at mesquite thorns,
spitting out the bladed hillsides' grit.

(2000)

THE SANCTIFICATIONIST OF AJO

Founder & ramrod, a proponent
of least said is soonest mended,
she bermed the soil, certain
the workings of the spirit transform us
into raised flower beds,
her sanctification a thorn in the flesh
of those husbands subject to root rot
& a face-saving semblance
of daytime control. Oh, that shadow war
on rooftops, every woman beholden
for small necessities, every man
an unflappable giant, striding
as if he owned the town.

(2000)

THE ORAL TRADITION
for Steve

Sometimes, in conversation,
he'll look away & say
I don't want to talk about it.
I respect that. I really do
but like some nosey Homeric hero
I can feel the words piling up
behind my teeth's barrier:
tell me, godammit! Tell me
everything so we can be friends!
I like to imagine the real
oral tradition, those epic heroes
all sitting around the cook fires,
gossiping, trading recipes, even
consoling one another as they
mend the horsehair plumes,
the helmets heavy in their laps.

(2010)

ABU GHRAIB (A TRUE STORY)

After 24 hours
nonstop rap, you
could hear them
in their cells,
calling "Whazzup,
whazzup, whazzup?"

         We
finally got it right.
Top 40 country,
one hour & they're
howling "Mister!
Mister! No more!"

     The blues, then,
for the ones we broke,
Arabic versions of "Help
the poor. Baby,
help poor me."

(2010)

DON'T GET ME STARTED

Last night at yoga
I listened to Elliot breathing
next to me like a patient
on a respirator. What if
there really is a soul?
Something the color
of duct tape or transparent
as plastic sheeting?
"Think about it," I say
at breakfast. My wife glares
& tries to hide behind the classifieds.
She's tired of my negative bullshit.
"Duct tape! Plastic sheeting!
Gee, I wonder why they're
pushing petroleum products?"
She leaves the table, her toast
untouched. Remember
chanting One! Two!
Three! Four! we don't
want your fucking war?
Remember that poster, girls say
yes to boys who say no?
I said to a girl across the room
what if they gave a war
& nobody came? I meant it,
it wasn't bullshit, but she untied

her macrame halter top anyway.
I like that slogan, no blood
for oil. Maybe I'll record it
on our answering machine or
shout it from our porch.
"You know," calls my wife
from the other room, "if you were
happier, you'd be happier."

(2010)

CHINA EXHIBIT

The plum wine goes well
with polite conversation:
your state shoes
should be black slippers,
your daily shoes
should be yellow canvas
like a speech's conclusion.
Tong, the potter,
threw himself into the kiln
with the impossible dragon bowls:
the firing was flawless.
Looking for the elixir of life,
the Taoist alchemists found
gunpowder, a conversation stopper
in any company.

(1993)

STEAM

I don't think Blake meant
you must create your own

style or be enslaved by another's.
I don't know emo from baby ho.

I do know corpse pose, how
to visualize myself as a body

of water. It's raining, the surface
of the lake steaming. I know

the true story of Jesse Owens.
Jesse, Jesse, he's our man!

Nigger, you can't sleep here.

(2010)

THE MUMMY

Wrapped in my blue & white striped
100% Egyptian cotton bed sheet,
I skulk in the vestibule. What a word–
ves.ti.bule, the last syllable
like breathing on a mirror. I overheard
two girls laughing about their teacher
arrested taking out the garbage
in his underwear. I say more power
to him. I'll say to those girls the night
I catch them, have a little mercy.
Mercy, a word that sounds
like someone swallowing flowers.

(2004)

THE FIRST SALTIST CHURCH OF TARIQ OUR LORD

Whenever my mother mentions
Jesus, I praise Tariq, how,
2000 years ago, his spaceship
crash landed in central Utah.
Tariq, the Prince of Saltus, Tariq,
the 10-foot-tall alien who talks to me
in my dreams, whose ship of salt
dissolved in the 100-year rain.
I pray twice a day, facing
the Great Salt Lake. I drink a glass
of salt water each night.
When this world of tears ends,
when Lord Tariq returns, the planet
Saltus blood-red on the horizon,
the faithful will be like unto salt crystals,
the sweat drying on his awful brow.
My proof? Look at our language.
"Salt of the earth," "salty dog,"
"the unplumbed, salt, estranging sea."
And tell me this: when it
rains, what pours?

(2007)

MY PRAYER

Martians, who believe everything
on earth is a machine, would wonder
about our new cat. Why do earthlings
keep a defective Geiger counter
around the house? Fundamentalists
believe something else~
the natural world is a work of art
marred by our sinful fingerprints.
Look at this sunset like a bad watercolor,
the sky littered with glass. Anyway,
Lord, whoever or whatever you are,
why don't you take off your starry crown
& drop by some morning for coffee?
I'd really like to chat.

(2004)

WASHING MACHINE

I give in,
bend down
& rest the side
of my head & then
my bare chest
on the lid
of the washing machine
lub-dubbing through
its rinse cycle.
Oh, heart & ear
attuned to a time-
saving appliance,
this porcelain drum
cycling moon
trash, moon
trash, moon
trash, a phrase
I'll hear for days.

(2010)

WHAT I DID IN HEAVEN

Flapped around. Practiced
safe sex. Egg white
instead of semen.

Yoga was the best,
the clouds breathing us,
every pose perfected,

I even did Vanquished Warrior,
that *asana* most women
on earth can do.

Can I come back now?

(2004)

HELEN

She's almost 90, her forehead
like an uncloudy day. She must've
been a beautiful baby. Now
she farts during yoga, plow pose,
cow-face pose, even corpse pose,
you can hear her backfiring like
an old Vespa among the scented
candles. Nobody laughs. Certainly
not me. No jokes about gasasana,
the five inner winds, the vibrations
of the blissful sheath. I'm practicing
ujaiyi breath, pretending I'm fogging
a mirror, imagining my blurred reflection,
which is almost nothing & preparing
to bow & say the divine in me
bows to the divine in you.

(2010)

About the Author

Jefferson Carter has lived in Tucson since 1954. Currently, he is a passionate volunteer with Sky Island Alliance, a locally-based environmental organization.

He has won a Tucson/Pima Arts Council Literary Arts Fellowship, and his poems have appeared in such publications as *Carolina Quarterly*, *Cream City Review*, *Cutthroat*, *Barrow Street*, *Sonora Review*, and *New Poets of the American West*. His chapbook *Tough Love* won the Riverstone Poetry Press Award. This is his ninth collection of poetry.

About Chax Press

Chax Press is a 501(c)(3) nonprofit organization, founded in 1984, that has published more than 130 books, including fine art editions and trade editions of literature and book arts works.

For more information, please see our web site at
http://chax.org

Chax Press is supported by individual contributions, and in part by the Tucson Pima Art Council and the Arizona Commission on the Arts, with funds from the State of Arizona and the National Endowment for the Arts.